MACRATH PUBLIC LIBRARY

D0646390

8/90
20.00

GO FOR IT!™

BASEBALL

FOR BOYS AND GIRLS

START RIGHT AND PLAY WELL

MAGRATH PUBLIC LIBRARY

by Bill Gutman

with Illustrations
by Ben Brown

SAUNDERS
BOOK COMPANY

GREY CASTLE PRESS

No part of this publication may be reproduced in whole or in part, or stored in a retrieval system, or transmitted in any form or by any means, electronic, mechanical, photocopying, recording, or otherwise, without written permission of Grey Castle Press.

Published by arrangement with Grey Castle Press, Lakeville, Ct.

Copyright © 1990 by Grey Castle Press.
Saunders Book Company
Canadian Library Edition

The *GO FOR IT* Sports Series is a trademark of Grey Castle Press.

Printed in the USA

The Library of Congress Cataloging in Publication Data

Gutman, Bill.
    Baseball : start right and play well / by Bill
Gutman ; with illustrations by Ben Brown.
        p.   cm. — (Go for it!)
    "Published by arrangement with Grey Castle Press, Lakeville, Ct."—
T.p. verso.
    Summary: Describes the history and current teams, leagues, and
championships of baseball and provides instruction on how to play
the game.
    ISBN 0-942545-84-2 (lib. bdg.)
    1. Baseball—Juvenile literature. [1. Baseball.] I. Brown,
Ben, 1921–   Ill. II. Title. III. Series: Gutman, Bill. Go for
it!
GV867.5.G88   1990
796.357'2—dc20   2677   89-7377
                                                                          CIP
                                                                          AC

Photo Credits: TV Sports Mailbag, pages 7, 8, 10, 11.

Special thanks to: John Lamb, former pitcher for the Pittsburgh Pirates.

Picture research: Omni Photo Communications, Inc.

Saunders Book Company
Canadian Library Edition
ISBN 1-895058-00-7

ABOUT THE AUTHOR

Bill Gutman is the author of over 70 books for children and young adults. The majority of his titles have dealt with sports, in both fiction and non-fiction, including "how-to" books. His name is well-known to librarians who make it their business to be informed about books of special interest to boys and reluctant readers. He lives in Poughquag, New York.

ABOUT THE ILLUSTRATOR

Ben Brown's experience ranges from cartoonist to gallery painter. He is a graduate of the High School of Music & Art in New York City and the University of Iowa Art School. He has been a member of the National Academy of Design and the Art Students' League. He has illustrated government training manuals for the disadvantaged (using sports as themes), and his animation work for the American Bible Society won two blue ribbons from the American Film Festival. He lives in Great Barrington, Massachusetts.

In order to keep the instructions in this book as simple as possible, the author has chosen in most cases to use "he" to signify both boys and girls.

A BRIEF HISTORY

No one can really say when man first used a bat or a club to hit an object through the air. Nor can anyone say for sure when this type of activity became a contest, or a game. But many feel that the forerunner of modern-day baseball might have been an English game called "stoolball," which was played several hundred years ago.

What is known is that a game similar to baseball was played in America during the nineteenth century. It slowly grew and began to look more and more like the sport we know today. A man named Alexander Cartwright wrote the first list of rules for baseball in 1845, and by 1869 there was a professional baseball team. It was called the Cincinnati Red Stockings, and in their first year the Red Stockings won 65 games and tied one.

Two years later, the first professional league was formed. It was called the National Association. The name was changed to the National League in 1876. The American League began in 1901. The two leagues made up major league baseball as we know it today.

The first World Series was played between the two leagues in 1903, the Boston Red Sox beating the Pittsburgh Pirates five games to three. The Series, played every fall, would become one of America's greatest sporting events.

There were many great players in the early years of baseball. Honus Wagner of Pittsburgh and Ty Cobb of Detroit were two of the best. Wagner was a shortstop, Cobb an outfielder. Two of the greatest pitchers of the day were Christy Mathewson of the New York Giants and Walter Johnson of the Washington Senators.

While there were still other fine players in that early time, baseball had a setback in 1919. That's when eight players on the Chicago White Sox took money to purposely lose the World Series to the Cincinnati Reds. Called the Black Sox Scandal, it was a low point in the game. But just then a man came along who helped put baseball back on top.

His name was George Herman Ruth, but everybody called him "Babe." Babe Ruth could hit the ball further than any player before him. He set a new home run record of 29 in 1919. A year later, he was traded from the Red Sox to the New York Yankees, and he belted 54 homers. In 1921, he hit 59, and the fans flocked to see him play.

Ruth started a new golden age of the game. He also helped to make the Yankees baseball's greatest team. More top players followed in the 1930s and into the 1940s, and many of them were sluggers. Players like Lou Gehrig, Jimmie Foxx, Hack Wilson, Hank Greenberg, Joe DiMaggio, Ted Williams and Ralph Kiner could all hit the ball a country mile.

The war years of 1941 to 1945 were tough ones for baseball. Many of the great players were in military service. But when the war ended, the game became bigger than ever. Then came 1947 and another milestone. That was the year Jackie Robinson of the Dodgers became the first black man to play in the major leagues.

Robinson broke the "color line" under very tough conditions. He became a Hall of Fame player because of his skills. But his courage also helped pave the way for all the great black players who followed.

In the 1950s, baseball's two great teams were the Yankees and the Brooklyn Dodgers. There were new superstars like Mickey

Babe Ruth

Mickey Mantle

Mantle of the Yankees, Willie Mays of the Giants, Henry Aaron and Warren Spahn of the Braves, Roy Campanella and Duke Snider of the Dodgers, Ernie Banks of the Cubs and Roberto Clemente of the Pirates.

There was another big change in 1958. That was the year the Dodgers and Giants moved to the West Coast. They became the Los Angeles Dodgers and San Francisco Giants. Now major league baseball stretched from coast to coast.

New ballparks were being built to hold more people, and new cities were getting big league teams for the first time. Several of the new stadiums had huge roofs, or domes. That made baseball an indoor game for the first time.

The 1960s and '70s marked the beginning of the modern era. The new players who had come into the game were breaking some of the greatest records ever set. Another group of modern-day sluggers would dominate the game.

Roger Maris hit 61 homers in 1961, breaking Ruth's mark of 60, while Henry Aaron finished his career with 755 home runs, also topping the Babe. Other power hitters were Willie Mays and Mickey Mantle, Eddie Mathews, Ernie Banks, Frank Robinson, Harmon Killebrew, Willie McCovey, Mike Schmidt and Reggie Jackson. There were also a number of great pitchers during the same era. Some of them were Sandy Koufax, Bob Gibson, Steve Carlton, Nolan Ryan, Tom Seaver, Jim Palmer, Catfish Hunter, Ferguson Jenkins and Don Drysdale.

In the 1980s, baseball continued to be the national pastime. New attendance records were set each year, and the players were earning huge amounts of money. Yet the top players continued to work hard at the game. Players such as Don Mattingly, Darryl Strawberry, Wade Boggs, Roger Clemens, Jose Canseco, Dwight Gooden, Frank Viola and Kirby Puckett were often compared to the players of the past.

Mike Schmidt

Reggie Jackson

And that's what makes baseball great. The game is never ending. Young people throughout the world are learning how to play. Some of them will be the stars of the future in a sport that millions of people truly love.

ORGANIZED BASEBALL

Baseball is a game for everyone. It can be played by both boys and girls, by both old and young. Any group of kids can get a ball, a bat, some gloves and find a field on which to play. But to really learn the game and be a better player, a boy or girl will probably want to play on a real team, and that team ought to be in an organized league.

When starting out in organized baseball, a player will be part of an amateur league. This means not getting paid to play. Players do this for fun and to learn the game. Little League, the Connie Mack League and the Babe Ruth League are examples of amateur baseball. So are the leagues in which college teams play.

But the really good players who want to make baseball a career go on to the professional leagues. They are now paid to pay baseball. The minor leagues and the major leagues are examples of professional baseball.

Most young professional players start out in the minor leagues. They don't make a great deal of money, but they have the chance to show that they are good enough for the major leagues. And if they reach the majors, they can make a great deal of money. Many of the best major league players today make more than a million dollars a year.

There are two major leagues, the American and the National leagues. Each league has an Eastern and Western Division. The

American League has seven teams in each division, while the National League has six in each. All the big-league teams can keep 24 players on the roster.

Big-league teams play 162 games a year. That's a lot of baseball, so the players must keep themselves in top condition. They must also travel a great deal, since there are professional teams from coast to coast and in Canada. At the end of each season, all four divisions will have a champion.

Then come the league play-offs. The two division winners in the American League play each other in a best of seven series, while the two National League champs do the same thing. The team that wins four games first is the pennant winner for that league and goes on to the World Series.

The World Series is professional baseball's greatest event. The two league champions play a best of seven series while the whole country watches. The winner is then the champion of the baseball world.

People have been playing baseball for more than 100 years. The two major leagues have been playing for more than 80 years. Today, baseball is bigger and better than ever at every level. Millions of people already play the game, with many more starting every year. The game is truly the national pastime.

LEARNING THE GAME

The Baseball Field

Everyone has heard a baseball field called a diamond. The diamond, however, is only the infield portion of the field. If you stand behind home plate and draw straight lines to first base, second base, third base and back home, the shape is like a diamond. Of course, if you look at it from between the bases, it will appear perfectly square.

The infield must always be the same size. In professional baseball, there are 90 feet between the bases. The bases are 15-inch-square white canvas bags, which must be between three and five inches thick. The pitching rubber is exactly 60 feet, six inches from the front of home plate. The rubber itself is 24 inches wide, while home plate, also made of hard white rubber, is 17 inches across. The front end is shaped like a square, the back like a diamond.

The batter's box, drawn with chalk lines, is six feet long and four feet wide. These dimensions are exactly the same at each and every professional field. A Little League field, however, will be smaller all around. But even in Little League, the infield, or diamond, must be the same at each field.

In the outfield, ballparks are often different. There is no set distance to the fences in left, center and right fields. In some ballparks, like Yankee Stadium in New York, left and left center field are much deeper than right and right center. In other parks, such as Riverfront Stadium in Cincinnati, the distances to left and right, left center and right center, are exactly the same. Many of the newer stadiums are built this way.

Every big-league field has a dugout where the players sit. Dugouts have sides and a roof. Most dugouts are slightly below ground level, though some of the newer ones are right at ground level. There is one dugout for the home team and another for the visitors.

The area in which the pitchers warm up is called the bull pen. The bull pen is sometimes located in foul territory near the outfield fence, or it can be beyond the fence. Relief pitchers and catchers will watch the game from the bull pen.

Every big-league park also has a scoreboard. Today, scoreboards are all electric. Many have big television screens to show pictures of the players or a replay of something that happened on the field. And, of course, the scoreboard tells you what is happening in the game (balls, strikes, runs, outs) and the scores of other games around the league.

One big difference among baseball fields is that some have real grass growing in the infield and outfield. Others now have artificial turf, which is almost like a carpet. All the indoor stadiums have artificial turf. But some outdoor stadiums also have artificial turf. In a few parks, the artificial turf covers the entire infield, except for a small area around the bases. In the past, the part of the infield where the fielders play and between the bases was always dirt. Today the players must adjust to a number of different kinds of fields.

Artificial turf has changed the game in a way. The ball moves faster on the carpet than on real grass, so teams that play in ballparks with artificial turf usually look for very fast fielders. But the artificial turf in the outdoor stadium gets very hot on a sunny summer day. Temperatures on the field can be as high as 120 degrees. For that reason, many players do not like playing on artificial turf.

On the other hand, the domed stadiums are air-conditioned in the summer. Baseball can be played in any weather. There are never any rain outs. For spectators, it's almost like watching a baseball game in their living rooms.

The Game

A major league baseball team consists of 24 players, a manager and several coaches. The manager is the boss. He makes all the decisions during a game. He also decides which players are in the starting line-up and who his pitcher will be.

The coaches all help the players to improve their games. They drill them in practice and will notice if a player is doing something wrong. A good coach can see if a pitcher isn't throwing the right way, or if a hitter is making a mistake at the plate.

A Little League or Babe Ruth team will usually have a head coach instead of a manager. Sometimes the coach will have one or two assistant coaches. But they must do many jobs. Most important is to teach the game correctly to young players, and that isn't always easy. To be a good player, a young person must learn the fundamentals of the game early and practice them often.

There are nine players on the field at one time. The pitcher always starts the action by throwing the ball to the catcher. There is a first baseman, a second baseman, a shortstop and a third baseman in the infield. The three outfielders are in left field, center field and right field.

Each position is different. There are special things that a youngster must learn in order to play a position well. Therefore, a boy or girl must decide which position he or she wants to play, then

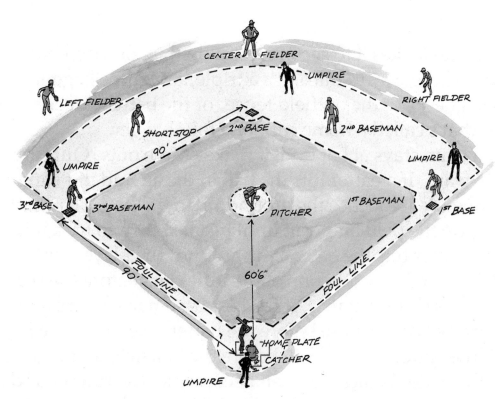

This is a basic baseball field showing the position of the players and umpires, as well as some of the distances. The outfielders, of course, normally play much deeper than shown here.

learn how to play it. Some players always play the same position. Others learn to play several positions. Sometimes it's good for a youngster to learn a number of different positions. Then, as he gets older, he can decide which one is best for him.

Every player must learn to hit. Some players hit from the right side of the plate, others from the left. A few players can hit from both sides. They are called switch hitters.

Hitters come to bat against the pitcher one by one. In each inning they must bat the same order. This is called the batting order, or line-up, and is decided by the coach or manager. The better hitters usually bat at the top of the order. But some coaches like to have a good hitter near the bottom, too. This balances the line-up.

The batters are trying to hit the ball past the fielders or between them. They are trying to get a hit. If the batter reaches first, it's a

17

single. If he makes it to second, it's a double, or a two-base hit. If he runs all the way to third, it's a triple, or a three bagger. And if the ball goes over the outfield fence, or the batter can circle all the bases, that's called a home run, or a four bagger.

Each team stays at bat until it makes three outs. Outs are made several ways. If a batter hits the ball in the air and it is caught by a fielder before it touches the ground, then he is out. The batter must leave the field and wait until his next turn to try again.

If the batter hits the ball on the ground, the player who fields the ball must throw it to one of the infielders before the runner reaches base. For instance, if the first baseman catches a throw with his foot on the base before the batter gets there, the batter is out. If the batter reaches first before the ball gets to the first baseman, the batter is safe. He then becomes a base runner and can stay on the base.

The batter doesn't have to swing at every pitch. If he lets a pitch go by, it will be called either a ball or a strike by the umpire. The umpire stands behind the catcher to call balls or strikes. A called strike is a pitch that passes over home plate between the batter's armpits and knees. A ball is a pitch that misses the plate inside or outside the strike zone or is too high or too low. If the batter hits a foul, it is also a strike. A swing and a miss is a strike as well. Three strikes and the batter is out. Four balls and he walks. This means he can go to first base.

Besides the home plate umpire, there are three other umps on the field, one for each base. They must decide whether balls are fair or foul and whether runners are safe or out on a close play at that base. People sometimes like to boo the umpires, but umps have a very important job.

When both teams have batted and made three outs, that means that one inning has been completed. A big-league game consists of nine innings. If a game is tied after nine innings, the teams must play extra innings until one team wins the game. Youngsters may be in leagues that play only six- or seven-inning games. Other than that, the same rules apply.

Learning How to Pitch

In some ways, pitching is the most important job on the team. Anyone can throw a baseball. But there is a great deal more to pitching than just throwing hard. It is the pitcher who puts the ball in play every time. Therefore, a pitcher will make many pitches during a ball game. The more good pitches he makes, the better chance his team has to win.

Since pitching is not a natural motion for the arm, a young pitcher must learn the correct way to throw the ball. Otherwise, he can hurt his arm, elbow or shoulder. In fact, many big-league pitchers have suffered from arm injuries during their careers.

To begin with, a pitcher must be in good physical condition. He must not only take care of his arm, but he also must keep the rest of his body in shape. A pitcher's legs, for example, are often just as important as his arm. He must use his legs to push hard off the mound and help drive his arm forward.

That's why most pitchers do a lot of running. Big-league pitchers run very often during spring training. Then they run between games during the season. They must also stretch to keep their leg muscles loose. No pitcher wants a pulled leg muscle.

A pitcher must throw with a comfortable, relaxed motion. Some prefer an overhand motion. Another might throw with a ''three-quarter'' motion, dropping his arm down lower as he releases the ball. Still others throw sidearm, and a very few pitch nearly underhand.

The worst thing a pitcher can do is to suddenly change his mo-

Left, Before starting your windup, you should feel comfortable and balanced on the mound. Concentrate on your catcher and look at your target—the catcher's mitt. You must have the proper grip on the ball and know just what kind of pitch you plan to throw.

Right, As you wind up, you should keep your eye on the catcher. Don't lose sight of his mitt. It is very important to have a smooth windup and to stay balanced. As you bring your front leg up (the kick), all your weight is on your back leg. Use that leg to thrust or push your body toward the plate. That leg drive helps you throw harder and put less strain on your arm.

tion. Throwing the ball a different way can lead to an arm injury. So if a certain way of throwing feels right to the young pitcher and doesn't put a strain on his arm, he should stick with it.

The kick is followed by the stride. Using your back leg for thrust, you should stride toward home plate. By this time, your arm is back in pitching position. As you stride, you will pivot with your hips and upper torso. Your arm follows, its movement following the flow of your body. Once again, the proper stride and pivot put less strain on your arm. By the time you snap your arm and release the ball, your stride has already added speed to your arm.

Another important part of pitching is control. A pitcher must be able to get the ball over the plate. He also has to be able to pitch to spots. That way he can ''work'' a hitter, throwing the ball inside or outside, high or low, whenever he wants. A pitcher with good control always has a better chance of getting the hitter out.

When there are no runners on base, a pitcher can take a full windup. There are a number of ways to do this. Some pitchers bring their arms over their heads. Others bring their arms only up to their chests. Still others simply pivot from the hip and throw. The young pitcher must decide which style is best. That means he must feel comfortable, keep his balance, push hard

Be sure to throw in a way that is most comfortable for you. Try to use an overhand or three-quarter motion. A smooth windup and stride will allow you to put less strain on your shoulder and throw with an easy motion. When you throw the basic fastball, you snap your wrist straight down as you release the ball off your fingertips.

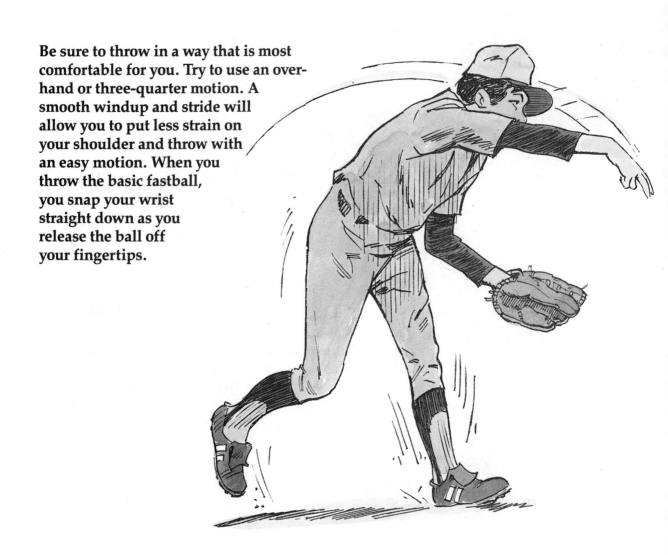

off his back leg and put as little strain on his pitching arm as possible.

The purpose of the windup and kick is for the pitcher to get the most out of his arm. Some pitchers use a high kick; others stride forward with their leg just off the ground. But both pivot and turn their bodies hard. The pitcher pivots from the third base side to the plate, if right-handed, and from the first base side to the plate, if left-handed.

As the pitcher pivots, he drives his hip and waist toward the plate. His arm follows, snapping or whipping the ball to the release point. A good pitcher will use the same windup and motion

The follow-through is a very important part of pitching. Your weight has now shifted to your front foot. Your arm has continued through its motion after the release of the ball. Your eyes should be riveted on home plate. You must also keep your body balanced so you can move quickly if the ball is hit back to you. This means shifting your weight back to both feet, standing square to the plate and holding your glove at chest level. You are now ready to field your position.

for every pitch. This makes it harder for the batter to guess what kind of pitch is coming.

When there is a runner on first or second base, the pitcher will use the stop or stretch position, instead of the full windup. This means he will stand sideways on the mound, facing the hitter. Before pitching, he must bring the ball and glove to his waist and

With runners on first or second, or on both first and second, a pitcher should come to a stop position. Instead of taking his regular windup, he stands sideways on the mound, facing the hitter. Before striding and throwing, he must bring the ball and glove to his waist and "stop" for a full second. The stop position allows a pitcher to keep base runners close to the bases. They are less likely to steal.

"stop" for a full second. He can then step off the rubber and throw to a base, or he can pivot and throw to home plate. The stop position keeps base runners from getting a big lead and easily stealing a base.

The completion of the pitching motion is called the follow-through. As the pitcher releases the ball, he must keep his arm moving through the throw. At the same time, he must bring his back leg around so his body is square to the plate. His glove hand is in front of his body, and he is ready to field his position if the ball is hit back to the mound.

Pitchers must always remember to warm up slowly. No one should throw real hard or "cut loose" the first few times he throws the ball. Throwing too hard, too soon, is another way a pitcher can hurt his arm.

What kinds of pitches should a young pitcher throw? The first rule for beginners is, don't get too fancy! Stick to basics. And that means a fastball and perhaps a change of pace. Neither pitch is likely to put any extra strain on a young person's elbow or shoulder.

The fastball is thrown straight and hard. Most pitchers grip the ball with their first two fingers on the seams. When they release it, the ball rolls off the tips of their fingers. Like all pitches, the fastball will be even better if the pitcher can control it. Then he can throw to the spot he wants. This is often called "location." A pitcher with good location is better able to "work" the hitter.

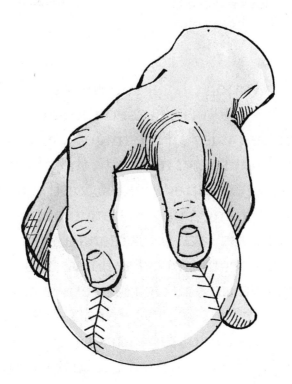

A fastball is held with the first two fingers on the seams. It is thrown hard and straight. When released, the fastball rolls off the tips of the fingers.

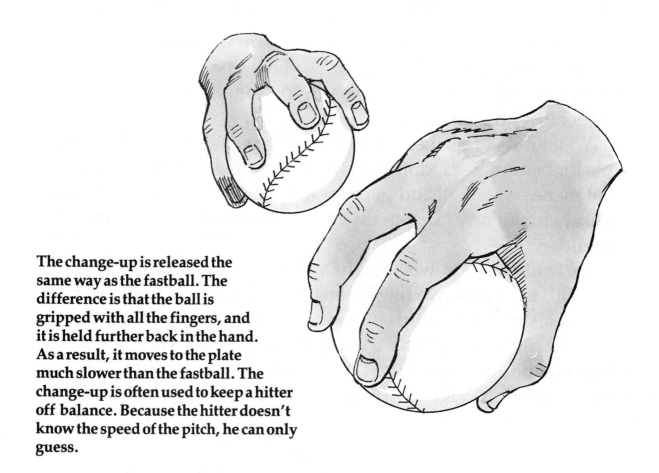

The change-up is released the same way as the fastball. The difference is that the ball is gripped with all the fingers, and it is held further back in the hand. As a result, it moves to the plate much slower than the fastball. The change-up is often used to keep a hitter off balance. Because the hitter doesn't know the speed of the pitch, he can only guess.

A second pitch a young player can throw is a change-up, or change of pace. This pitch is released the same way as a fastball. But the ball is gripped with all the fingers, and it is held further back in the hand. That way it moves to the plate much more slowly than a fastball. A hitter looking for the fastball can really be fooled by a good change-up or change of pace.

Once young pitchers reach their teens and their arms are more developed, they can begin throwing curve balls. A curve ball is held with the first two fingers close together and across the seams. As the pitcher releases it, he snaps his wrist outward and lets the ball roll off the top of his index finger. The rotation of the ball catches the air currents, which cause it to curve or "break" as it comes to the plate. A right-hander's curve moves from right to left, while the lefty's moves from left to right.

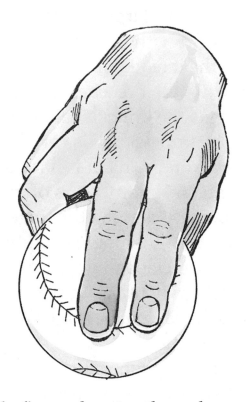

To throw a curve, place the fingers closer together and across the seams. The pitch is released with an outward snap of the wrists and the ball rolls off the top of the index finger.

A pitch that has become more popular today is the slider. It is held and thrown much like the curve, only harder. This leads to a quicker and later break on the ball, making it a pitch that often fools hitters. But like the curve, the slider can put a great deal of strain on the arm of a young pitcher.

Some pitchers throw a screwball. This is really a reverse curve. To throw it, a pitcher snaps his wrist inward and lets the ball roll off his middle finger. But the screwball, or "scroogie," can put even more strain on the elbow and can shorten a pitcher's career, even a major leaguer's. So young players must be very careful about throwing the screwball.

There are still other pitches that can be used by older hurlers. One that is becoming popular today is the split-fingered fastball.

For this, a pitcher must have a large hand with long fingers, because the ball must be held with the fingers spread wide apart. The ball is released off the inside of the fingers, instead of the tips, and often dips sharply just as it reaches the plate.

Another special pitch is the knuckleball. It is sometimes called a floater or flutterball. The knuckleball is very hard to control because it moves in several directions. It is hard to say which way it will go. Therefore, it can take many years of practice to learn the pitch. It is usually thrown by digging the fingernails of the first two fingers into the ball and pushing it straight out upon release.

Thrown this way, the knuckleball floats, rather than spins, and the air currents can really play tricks with it. Knuckleballs are not thrown hard, and knuckleball pitchers rarely have arm trouble. They can pitch for a long time.

The longer a young player pitches, the more he or she will learn about pitching. It is a real art. The pitcher will gradually learn how to work the hitters. He will learn that if he keeps the ball low, the batter will more than likely hit it on the ground. If the ball is kept high, it will often be popped into the air.

The pitcher will also learn which batters can be fooled with the change-up, and which ones will swing at a low, outside curve. And he'll learn that to be a good pitcher, it is necessary to remain cool. Even with the bases loaded, a pitcher must not get rattled. He has to bear down, but still pitch his game, throw easily, follow through, and be ready for anything.

When he can do that, he has become real pitcher.

Learning How to Field

A pitcher is only as good as the fielders behind him. Since no pitcher is going to strike out every batter, the fielders are going to play a big role in the outcome of every ball game. A key error can lose a ball game, but a great fielding play can save one.

Fielders must also know the game situation at all times. They have to know when to try for a double play, when to throw to the cutoff man, when to expect a bunt, when to look for a steal or a hit-and-run play. In other words, the fielders must be very alert at all times.

Let's see what it takes to play each position on the ball field.

The Catcher

The catcher plays a very tough position. Because a catcher must squat down and get up maybe hundreds of times in a game, he has to be strong and durable. He also must be able to stand up to an occasional collision at home plate with a charging base runner.

Because it can be dangerous behind home plate, catchers wear masks, chest protectors and shin guards. And they still often get hit by foul balls. A good catcher can't let any of this bother him because he has to be aware of what's happening in the game at all times. The catcher is almost like a coach on the field.

First of all, he must ''call'' the game for the pitcher. That means he tells the pitcher what kind of pitch to throw by signaling him with his hand. To do that right, the catcher must know the batting habits of the hitters. If a certain hitter likes to hit low pitches, the catcher will call for pitches that are near the top of the strike zone. If the hitter can be fooled by the change-up, the catcher must know how to set him up for that pitch.

He must also have a strong and quick arm. If a runner tries to

The catcher must always give the pitcher a strong target with his glove. The glove shows the pitcher where he should throw the ball. With today's big, hinged mitts, a catcher might tuck his bare hand behind his leg to protect it from foul tips. He will then catch the ball one-handed. But this takes practice.

steal a base, the catcher must spring up from his squatting position and fire the ball to second or third. He must also be quick enough to jump out from behind the plate to field bunts. And he has to be able to locate and catch high foul pops. All of this takes a great deal of practice.

The catcher also has to remind his fielders when there are one or two outs. He must make sure they know where to throw the ball in a certain game situation. It's no wonder that the catcher is very tired at the end of every game.

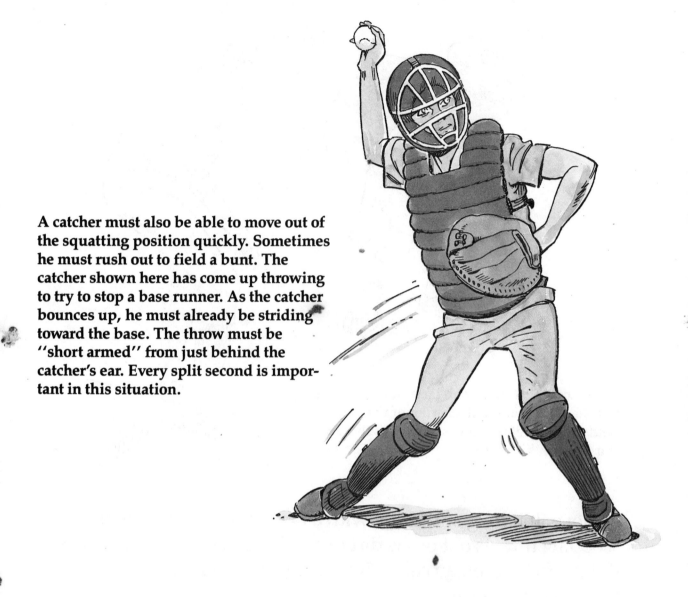

A catcher must also be able to move out of the squatting position quickly. Sometimes he must rush out to field a bunt. The catcher shown here has come up throwing to try to stop a base runner. As the catcher bounces up, he must already be striding toward the base. The throw must be "short armed" from just behind the catcher's ear. Every split second is important in this situation.

First Baseman

A first baseman has to know his or her position very well. During a game, he will take many throws from his infielders. Some will be high, others in the dirt, some to the right and others to the left. The first baseman must be able to catch them all, and he has to always do it with one foot on the bag.

To help him catch the ball, the first baseman has a special kind

When holding a runner on base, the first baseman stands square to the corner of the bag. He
bends slightly at the knees and gives the pitcher
a target with his glove.

of glove. It is long and large, with a deep pocket. This helps when
scooping throws out of the dirt or reaching for very high throws.
But the first baseman can't always rely on his glove. He must
know what to do at all times.

When a ground ball is hit to another infielder, the first baseman
runs quickly to the bag. He must then stand squarely in front of
the base, ready to move in any direction for the throw. To do this,
he must be prepared to quickly shift his feet.

For example, if a throw is made to the home plate side of the
base, a right-handed first baseman would put his right foot on the
corner of the bag and stretch out with his left leg and left hand. A
left-handed first baseman would put his left foot on the corner of

The first baseman must learn to "stretch" for a throw. He must judge where the ball is coming to him, and then place the proper foot on the corner of the bag. Then he must reach as far toward the incoming throw as he can. A good stretch can make the difference between an out or a safe call on a play.

the bag and stretch out with his right leg and right hand for the same throw.

It takes long hours of practice and thousands of throws for a first baseman to really feel good around the bag. He must get so that his moves and footwork come naturally. That way, he's always ready for anything.

The first baseman must also be able to field ground balls. If there is a runner on first, he often will "hold" the runner by standing on the bag and waiting for a pickoff throw from the pitcher. Seeing this, the runner is not likely to move very far from the bag. In addition, the first baseman must work with the catcher on high pop-ups between home and first, and he must learn to make a "sweep" tag when a high throw pulls him off the bag.

Some people think a left-handed player makes a better first

baseman. That's because he can throw to any of the other bases without shifting his feet. That may be true, but there have been many very good right-handed first sackers as well. As with every other position, it takes hard work and practice.

Second Baseman

The second baseman plays between first and second base most of the time. He or she must have speed and quickness to move to the right or left. He must also be able to cover second base on some steal attempts and tag plays, as well as cover first when the first baseman charges a bunt.

Many times, the second baseman is a small, quick player. His arm doesn't have to be as strong as the shortstop's or third baseman's. But he sometimes has to make a tough throw from second or double plays.

Like all the other infielders, the second baseman must practice fielding ground balls. It is usually better for the infielder to charge a ground ball. If he backs up on it, the runner will have a better chance of beating the throw. Backing up is often called ''letting a ball play you.''

The second baseman must also learn to position himself in front of the bag on tag plays. Like the first baseman, he should stand squarely in front of the bag. That way he can be ready to move in either direction for the throw. He must be careful to avoid the spikes of a sliding runner. But he has to be sure to tag the runner before the runner's hand or foot reaches the base.

Perhaps the hardest skill for the second baseman to learn is the double play. With a runner on first, any ball hit to the infield is a possible double play. If it is hit to the second baseman, he has to time his throw to the shortstop, who is covering second. He must

34

Like the other infielders, the second baseman should keep his glove low when fielding ground balls. He should also begin moving toward first just before the ball hits his glove. That way he can throw in one, smooth motion.

make sure the ball gets to the bag just as the shortstop is crossing it. That way the shortstop can grab the ball, avoid the runner and fire the ball to first to take out the hitter.

If the ball is hit to shortstop or third base, then the second baseman must make the pivot play. The pivot may be the toughest single thing the second baseman has to do. He must run to the bag and face the shortstop or third baseman, who will throw the ball to him. After catching the ball while on the bag, he must pivot and throw quickly to first. Many times, the base runner coming in will try to make it harder for him to throw by sliding right into

A second baseman must be able to "turn" a double play. That often means making a relay throw to first as a base runner is sliding into the base. This kind of "pivot and throw" takes a lot of practice.

him. A good second baseman must be able to leap over a sliding runner while throwing to first at the same time. To be able to do this well takes many, many hours of practice.

The Shortstop

A shortstop plays between second and third and must be a fast player who can cover a lot of ground to both his or her right and left. He must also have a strong throwing arm. He will sometimes have to make long throws to first from deep short, nearly behind third. He will also have to throw while off balance, sometimes while spinning around or even from his knees.

Every good team has a good shortstop. To become a good shortstop, a young player must practice a great deal. He must field hundreds of ground balls and work on his throwing. Like the other infielders, a shortstop will get in a crouch with his glove held low just before the ball is pitched.

Then, as the pitch reaches the plate, the shortstop rocks forward onto the balls of his feet. That way he can move quickly to his left or right. A good infielder will try to take a ground ball as

As the ball is pitched, the shortstop and all other infielders must be ready to move quickly to the right or left. To do this, infielders must bend at the knees, keep their gloves down and rock forward on the balls of their feet just as the ball is pitched.

he begins his move toward first base. If he does that, he can go into his throwing motion without losing any time, since he is already moving in that direction.

All infielders usually throw both overhand and sidearm. If a shortstop has to backhand a ball going to his right, he will have to plant his right foot and throw overhand. That way he can make a strong throw. If he has to charge in for a ball, he will often throw sidearm to get the ball away faster.

The shortstop must also be able to tag runners at second on steal attempts and must be able to "turn" the double play. He doesn't have to pivot, but he must practice taking the throw from his second baseman just as he crosses the bag. He must often throw to first while avoiding the sliding base runner.

The shortstop must sometimes backhand a ball in the "hole" between short and third. To make this play, he must be quick and sure-handed. Once he has caught the ball, he must stop, set his feet and make a hard, overhand throw to first.

A good shortstop will also move back to catch pop flies. If the ball is directly over his head, he can backpedal to catch it. But if it is to his right or left, he must run sideways as he watches the ball. Sometimes the shortstop will have to run behind the third baseman and catch a pop-up in foul territory.

A good shortstop must do many things. He may be the most important infielder of them all. It takes a lot of hard work and practice to become a good shortstop.

Third Baseman

The third baseman must have the strongest throwing arm of any of the infielders. He or she usually has the longest throw to first base and sometimes has to throw while off balance, from his knees, or even from a sitting position. In addition, he has to be very quick, while moving to his left or right, because balls are often hit to him very hard. For that reason, third base is sometimes called the ''hot corner.''

A third baseman must know where to play at all times. If he thinks a hitter may bunt, he must play in close, well in front of the bag. He also has to be able to charge a bunt, pick it up bare-handed and throw it sidearm to first. At other times, he will play behind the bag and close to the foul line. Then he can stop a ball from being hit between him and the bag.

There are times when a ball will be hit so hard that the third baseman will have to dive to his right or left to catch it. That's when he may have to make a throw from his knees, or get to his feet very quickly to throw. All this takes a lot of practice.

A player can't be afraid of the ball if he plays third. There are times when a third baseman will have to stop a hard-hit ball with his body, then pick it up and throw. Like the other infielders, he must be able to move back on a pop-up, or catch foul pops near

A third baseman must be very alert, since balls can come to the "hot corner" quickly. Sometimes a third sacker will have to dive through the air to try to stop the ball.

the stands. An infielder getting ready to catch a pop-up should "call" it. By yelling, "I got it," he is telling another fielder to back off. Otherwise, there might be a collision and no one will make the catch.

All the infielders must also know how to take a cutoff throw from the outfield. If an outfielder has to field a ball in the deepest part of the ballpark, he might not be able to throw to third or home. Seeing the play develop, an infielder will run out toward the outfielder. As the outfielder turns, the infielder will hold his arms up, showing that he is the cutoff man. Then the outfielder can throw the ball to the infielder, who will whirl and relay the ball to the base the runner is trying to reach.

Each of the four infield positions takes time to learn to play well. Some infielders can play all the positions. They are called "utility" infielders. But if a player likes one of the positions best, then he should practice the special things that will make him as good as he can be.

Learning To Play
The Outfield

Playing the outfield may look easier than playing the infield, but it isn't. An outfielder may not be as busy during a game, but all of a sudden he or she may have to make a play that could mean winning or losing the ball game.

There are three outfielders—the left fielder, the right fielder and the center fielder. Of the three, the center fielder is usually the fastest. He has the largest area to cover, since center field is always the deepest part of the ballpark. So the center fielder must be able to move back on long flies and come in for short ones. He must also be able to catch balls in the gaps to his right or left.

The left and right fielders do not have to cover as much ground. But they still must know how to play their positions well. They have to know how to go after fly balls along the foul line, where they will be running dangerously close to the stands. In addition, they must know how to "play the angles" down the foul lines. There, balls often hit the wall in the corner and bounce out quickly. A good fielder is able to judge where the ball will go after it bounces. The center fielder and right fielder usually have the strongest throwing arms, but all the outfielders must be able to make long throws to home plate.

Whenever possible, outfielders should catch fly balls with two hands. A one-handed catch may look showy, but there is a greater chance of dropping the ball. A young outfielder should keep his eye on a fly ball at all times. The best big-league outfielders can sometimes take a glance at the wall or another outfielder without losing the ball. But it takes years of practice to do that. Also, an outfielder should not forget to yell, "I got it," when the ball is hit between him and another outfielder.

An outfielder must throw the ball on a straight line. If he makes a high, lazy throw, it will take too long to reach the base. Some-

An outfielder should catch a routine fly ball with two hands. To make the catch, he should be directly below the descending ball, hold his glove above eye level and cover the glove with his bare hand as soon as the ball hits it.

times an outfielder's throw will bounce once or twice. That's all right, as long as the throw is accurate. But whenever an outfielder fields a ball with runners on base, he has to try to be in a position to throw.

All outfielders will sometimes have to run back for a ball. The correct way for the fielder to do this is to retreat while looking over his shoulder at the flight of the ball. With more practice, an outfielder will learn how to take his eyes off the ball for a second to check for the fence or another fielder, then return his eyes to the ball again.

When an outfielder knows he has to make a throw, he should hang back on a fly ball until the last instant. Then, just before catching it, he should take a step forward so he is already moving to home plate. This makes it easier for him to stride and throw. Because of the throws they must make, outfielders almost always throw overhanded.

Outfielders must also back each other up. If the left fielder is running to cut off a ball in the gap, the center fielder must run behind him in case the ball gets through. On base hits, the outfielder must charge the ball and pick it up quickly. If he waits for the ball to come to him, the runner might take an extra base.

Knowing the hitters is also important to an outfielder. If a right-handed batter is a "pull" hitter, the outfielders can "shade" the hitter to left. That means the left fielder will play close to the line, the center fielder will play toward left center, and the right fielder will play toward right center. Knowing the hitters gives the outfielder a better chance to catch fly balls and cut off hits in the gaps.

Since the outfields in all ballparks are different, a good outfielder will always know where he is. He will know how to play a ball off a high wall as well as off a low fence. He will know how far he can run before he hits the wall. And he must know where the fences are padded and where they are not. Knowing all these things can help an outfielder win a ball game, and also keep him from getting hurt.

Every position on a baseball team is important. A poor fielder will hurt his team sooner or later, no matter where he plays. If a boy or girl wants to play baseball, he or she has to be able to field, whether as a first baseman, a catcher or an outfielder. Each position is different, but each has common skills. Good fielding takes practice, and every player, young or old, must work hard to get better.

Learning to Hit

Hitting a baseball may be the hardest single skill to master in all of sports. Even the best hitters never stop practicing. They practice hitting the ball to right field, then to left field, then up the middle. Then they practice hitting high pitches and low pitches, fastballs and curves.

This is also what a young hitter must do. He or she should practice hitting from the first time he picks up a bat. To begin

The outlined area above home plate is the strike zone. Any pitched ball passing through this area will be called a strike by the plate umpire. When a pitcher is "working the corners," he is trying to throw the ball right on the edges of the strike zone.

with, he must find the right bat, one that is not too heavy. Then he has to have a comfortable batting stance at the plate while waiting for the pitch.

There is no right or wrong batting stance. In fact, there are as many different stances as there are players. The important thing is to feel comfortable in the batter's box, be able to see the ball well, then take a good, level swing. A young player might be smart to begin with a "square" stance and take it from there.

A young player should start with a comfortable batting stance. He should stand midway in the batter's box, with his feet spread slightly apart. The batter's arms are held away from his body, and he should bend slightly at the knees, holding the bat at an angle just above the shoulder.

That means he should stand in the middle of the batter's box, feet spread slightly apart. If the front foot is closer to home plate, it is a "closed" stance. If the front foot is away from home plate, it is an "open" stance.

The batter should bend slightly at the knees so he can move quickly. He should hold his arms away from his body and his bat at an angle just above the shoulder. As the pitcher delivers the ball, the batter will stride forward with his front leg, extend his arms back, then pivot at the hips. The bat will follow, with first the arms and then the wrists snapping the bat into the ball.

The batter must always watch the pitcher closely. When he starts to throw, the batter will stride forward with his front leg and extend his arms back. He is now ready to pivot and swing.

Besides a comfortable stance, a young hitter should work on a level swing. To try to uppercut the ball or chop down on it is not the right way to become a good hitter. If the batter hits the center of the ball with a level swing, the ball should travel straight off the bat. That kind of hit is a line drive, and some of the best hitters in baseball are line-drive hitters.

A level swing can also produce other kinds of hits. If the batter takes a level swing but makes contact below the center of the ball, the ball will rise as it leaves the bat. It will be either a pop-up if it is

The batter follows his stride by pivoting at the hips. This movement creates momentum for the swing. The bat follows the hips, with the arms moving first. Then the wrist snaps the bat through the contact point. It is very important for a young player to develop a level swing. That way he is less likely to develop bad habits.

hit very low, or a fly ball if it is hit just below the center. And if the batter hits it real hard just below the center of the ball, it just might be a home run!

On the other hand, if the batter takes a level swing but hits the ball above the center, it will head downward. That is a ground ball, or grounder. Like line drives and fly balls, grounders can be either hits or outs. It all depends on where the ball goes.

This is something else a good hitter can do. He can hit the ball to any field. If a batter makes contact just as the ball is going past him, he will hit it back up the middle of the field. But if he swings a split second early and catches the ball before it goes past him, he will "pull" the ball. This means a right-handed hitter will hit to the left field, and a left-handed hitter will hit to right field.

As with most swinging motions, the follow-through is also an important part of hitting. The batter must be sure to finish his swing by turning his wrists over and completely swinging through the ball before beginning to run.

But if the hitter swings a split second late and connects with the ball when it has gone a bit past him, he will hit it to the opposite field. This means a right-handed hitter will hit it to right field, and a left-handed hitter to left field. There are times when a good hitter will try to pull, or maybe hit, to the opposite field.

A batter must also decide what kind of swing he wants to take. Big, strong players who hit a lot of home runs often take big swings. They can hit the ball further that way, but they also miss more often. So a big swinger will strike out quite a bit.

Hitters who look for singles and doubles often take a shorter, more compact swing. They feel that kind of swing gives them more control of the bat. Instead of bolding the bat down at the end, they often hold it a few inches up the handle. This is called choking up. Choke hitters will often get a piece of the ball and won't strike out too often. That's why they have a better chance to get a hit.

A young player shouldn't try to be a slugger right away and go for a home run with each pitch. He should learn to hit first, to handle the bat. Then, if he grows bigger and stronger and finds he can hit the ball a long way, he can begin to take a bigger cut.

One other thing a hitter must learn to do is bunt. Though bunting may seem like a little thing, a good bunt can sometimes be the difference between winning and losing. And there are not that many good bunters in baseball today.

To bunt, a player will slide his top hand halfway up the bat and turn to face the pitcher. This is called squaring around. He holds the bat loosely in his hands and doesn't really swing at the ball. He just lets the ball hit the bat and bounce off, so it does not go very far. The batter will try to bunt away from the fielders. Sometimes he will push the ball toward first. Other times, he may bunt toward third. There are also times when a hitter won't square to bunt. He will try to drop the ball down in front of home plate as he starts running to first base.

A player uses this style when he is bunting for a base hit, trying to place the ball in front of or between the fielders. He will then try to reach first before the fielder can throw him out. Other times, he may make a ''sacrifice'' bunt. That means he is bunting to get a base runner from first to second, or second to third. If the bunt is made correctly, the fielder cannot throw out the runner, only the hitter. A good sacrifice bunt can often lead to a run. The batter usually squares around on a sacrifice bunt.

Another time the bunt is used is on the ''squeeze play.'' A player may bunt with a runner on third base and his team needing one run. So the batter is bunting to get the runner home from

A batter bunting the ball should square off and face the pitcher. He must then slide his top hand halfway up the bat, holding it loosely in his hands. The trick is to let the ball hit the bat and bounce off and not try to hit it with the bat. A good bunter can place the ball just where he wants it to go.

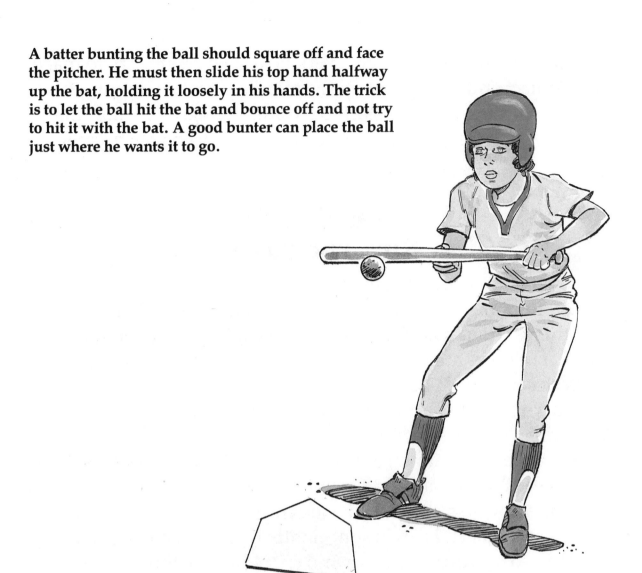

third. If the runner breaks with the pitch, it's called a "suicide squeeze." If he waits to see where the ball is bunted, it's called a "safety squeeze." Either way, the squeeze needs a good bunt in order to work.

Bunting has been a part of baseball for many, many years. All young players must learn to lay a bunt down.

After a young person has played the game for a while, he or she might want to try different batting stances and different styles of hitting. But for beginners, it is still best to start with fundamentals. Get a comfortable stance. Work on a level swing. Try to make solid contact and hit the ball up the middle. Practice bunting. Then, slowly, a player can start to try other things. But most importantly, a player should practice hitting every chance he gets.

Learning To Run The Bases

The player who can run the fastest is not always the best base runner. Running the bases is not as easy as it looks. There are even things to learn about simply circling all the bases at full speed. The sacks are 90 feet apart in the big leagues. They are much closer in Little League. The bases, except for home plate, are square bags above the ground. A sloppy base runner can easily trip over a base and fall.

For a good base runner, a trip around the bases looks effortless. He cuts each bag easily and never breaks stride or slows down. He knows how to step on the inside corner of each bag and push off toward the next. He will run slightly wide of each bag before he hits it, so his turn is smooth and crisp, but not too sharp.

The base runner must also stay within the baselines. That is, he cannot zigzag in and out or run very wide to avoid a tag. The foul lines go to first and third base, and there is an imaginary line between first and second, and second and third. It is the umpire who will judge when a player has run out of the baselines.

The only base a runner can go past without being tagged out is first. On a ground ball, he can run right past the bag, and if he beats the throw, he can then turn and walk back to the base. But he must make his turn toward foul territory. If he turns the other way as if he is going to run to second, then he can be tagged.

A good base runner will also practice making quick starts and stops. This is very important, especially when trying to steal a base, or starting on a hit-and-run play. Also, besides practicing quickness, the young base runner will also have to learn how to slide.

There are a number of slides a base runner can use. The simplest is the straight in, or pop-up slide. The runner will come into the base at full speed. When he is close enough, he will start his slide by putting one leg out in front of him and folding the other under it. Then when his front foot hits the bag, he uses the other leg to push himself back to a standing position. That's why it's called the pop-up slide.

A player may also slide straight in without folding the second leg under the first. It is the same slide, only he won't pop back up to a standing position.

A runner using the "pop-up" slide goes straight for the base. His lower leg is folded under him at the knee and will allow him to push himself back to a standing position once his front leg hits the bag. This way he's ready to run again if the throw is wild. It is also a good idea to keep the lead foot an inch or two off the ground. This will prevent the runner's spikes from digging into the dirt and causing an ankle injury.

Other runners prefer to slide head first. The headfirst slide always looks exciting. As the runner nears the bag, he simply dives headfirst, touching the base with his hands rather than his feet. Runners who slide headfirst feel they can get to the bag quicker. But they also risk injury. A player can hurt his hand, or he can be tagged in the face with the ball. He will also take a beating on his

The hook slide takes a lot of practice. The runner should slide to the outside of the base and hook the bag with his trailing foot. This way he might avoid the tag on a close play. The runner should also try to keep his fists closed to avoid injury to the fingers.

chest and stomach. Still, many runners will use the headfirst slide as their only one.

Perhaps the toughest slide is the hook slide. As he nears the base, the runner slides to one side or the other, then hooks the base with his trailing leg, which is bent under him, as with the pop-up slide. Some runners feel the hook slide helps them to avoid the tag. But the slide is also hard on the body and can lead to very sore legs and thighs if used all the time.

The fall-away slide is similar to the hook. The runner falls away from the bag as he begins his slide and catches the base with his trailing foot, which is bent outward. It is another tough slide to master.

Base runners will slide when they try to steal a base or when the play is close. They know they must slide when they steal. On plays at third and home, the coach or the next batter will usually signal the runner to slide. They have a better view of the play and know if it will be close. If they hold their hands high in the air, the batter knows he can come in standing up. But if they hold their hands low, palms down, the runner had better slide.

A good base runner must know his own speed, as well as the arm strength of the outfielders. That way he can judge whether to try to stretch a single into a double or to try to go from first to third on a base hit. He must also decide whether to tag up and try for an extra base on a fly ball.

A good base runner can also learn how to steal bases. Base stealers are usually fast runners, but there are tricks to stealing that every young player can learn.

The four most important things are the lead, reading the pitcher, the jump and the slide. The base runner must take as big a lead as he can and still be able to get back to the bag if the pitcher tries to throw him out. When taking a lead, the runner should keep his feet apart, crouch down, let his hands hang in

When leading off a base, the runner must be ready to move quickly in either direction. The best way for him to do this is to bend at the waist and knees. He can then let his arms hang down loosely in front of him and get on the balls of his feet when the pitcher begins his motion. The runner should watch the pitcher at all times.

front and watch the pitcher. This way he is ready to spring in either direction.

Reading the pitcher means knowing his motion. Then the runner can take off the moment he is sure the pitcher is really going to pitch and not try to pick the runner off. If the runner only guesses, he might very well get picked off. So he should always watch the pitcher, even when not on base. He may see something that will later allow him to steal.

The jump, or quick start, and the slide we have already talked about. But in stealing, the quick start is very important. A runner who is going full speed after three steps has a better chance than a runner who takes six steps to reach speed, even if the second man is faster. And a good slide can sometimes mean the difference between being out and being safe.

There are times when a stolen base can mean a ball game. So even if a player's not the fastest person on the team, he should know the fundamentals of stealing. Because in baseball, you never know what might happen.

Good baserunning is yet another way to win baseball games. At the same time, poor baserunning can cost runs and ball games. Even if a player is already a good hitter and a good fielder, he must still become a good base runner. Only then will he be a complete player.

Keeping Yourself And Your Equipment Fit

Once you decide to join a baseball team, you are making a commitment. This means you will always do your best to help yourself and your teammates. Part of that commitment is to always be ready to play. This means coming to practices and games on time. You have to be sure to get enough sleep so you can do your best on the field, and to eat the right foods so your body is ready to play the game.

Most young players need at least eight hours of sleep or more. This is especially true the night before a game. If you're tired, you are more likely to make a mistake on the field. And you may also run out of gas in the late innings when the game is on the line. So sleep is very important.

So is eating the right foods. You should not eat too many junk foods anyway. Fresh fruits, juices, meat, vegetables, rice, pasta are all things that are good for you. Too much soda, candy, cake, fried foods and hot dogs will not help you become bigger and

All baseball players must always be in good physical condition. It is important to exercise before, during and after the season. A good coach will show his team the proper exercises to do.

stronger. It is especially important not to eat a lot of these things before a ball game. No one can play well on a full stomach.

And, needless to say, you should never smoke cigarettes, drink alcoholic beverages or take any kind of drugs. Be smart and say no.

You should also keep your body fit by doing extra running, as well as strength and stretching exercises. Just playing baseball isn't enough, because much of the time you are just standing around. You sit in the dugout between innings, or stand in the field waiting for a ball to be hit to you. Unless you are the pitcher or catcher, a game can sometimes be slow.

So you must run between games, do push ups and sit-ups, plus a lot of stretching. You can also become involved in a weight-training program, if you have someone to show you the right way and the best exercises.

58

Stretching the leg and arm muscles is also important. There are a lot of quick starts and stops in the field and on the bases. If you don't keep your muscles loose by stretching, you can easily pull a muscle and be out of action.

You should also warm up your throwing arm, even if you are not a pitcher. An outfielder sometimes has to make a long, hard throw to the infield or home plate. If his arm is not warm, he can hurt it. That's why both infielders and outfielders throw a ball around before every inning.

Batters, too, must stretch before hitting so they don't pull a muscle. While waiting in the on-deck circle for your turn at bat, you should loosen your arms by stretching and swinging a weighted bat around. Then take a number of practice cuts before you come to the plate. That way you'll be ready.

Taking care of your equipment and uniform requires some old-fashioned common sense. Bats and gloves should never be allowed to stay wet or dirty. They should always be wiped down after a ball game and dried. Gloves should be treated every few weeks with linseed oil or another kind of dressing that keeps leather soft and pliable. That way the leather won't crack.

You must also make sure the lacing on your glove is in good shape. You wouldn't want a lace to break during a game or while you're trying to make a catch. If the lacing looks bad, have the glove restrung.

Use your bat to hit a baseball and nothing else. If you go home and begin hitting stones in the backyard, your bat will get nicked and dented. And it might break. Even aluminum bats are not made to hit stones or other objects. With an aluminum bat, you must make sure the rubber grip is in good shape. Otherwise, it should be replaced.

Uniforms should be kept clean at all times. You just won't look very good if you start the game with a dirty and wrinkled uni-

To become a good player takes patience and practice. But if a boy or girl learns the right way to play, to hit, to run and to throw, he or she can have fun, play well and maybe even be a hero.

form. You should also keep your cleats cleaned and polished. Remove the dirt in the cleats after each game or practice. Wipe your shoes down, check the laces, and if your shoes need polishing, do it. Then your shoes will last a lot longer. If you outgrow them, you can still give them to your little brother or sister, or to a friend.

All of these things are part of the game. A strong, healthy player is a better player. A player who takes care of his bat, glove and uniform will be more confident. He knows he is ready to go out there and get that clutch base hit, make that great catch, get that key strike-out or steal that big base. This is what makes a winner, a player who is always ready to go for it when the game is on the line.

Glossary

Batter's Box A 4′ by 6′ chalk-lined box on both sides of home plate. Batters must stand in this box when hitting.

Bull Pen An area just outside the playing field where pitchers can warm up during a ballgame.

Bunt To hit the ball very softly so it rolls a short distance from home plate.

Choke Hitter A player who holds his hands several inches up from the end of the bat.

Closed Stance A batting stance in which the hitter's front foot is closer to home plate than his rear foot.

Control (see **Location**) Term used to describe a pitcher's ability to get the ball over the plate in the strike zone.

Cutoff Man The middle man, usually an infielder, on a long throw. This player in turn relays the ball to the appropriate base.

Diamond The nickname for the infield portion of a baseball field.

Doubleplay A single play that results in two members of the team at bat being called out.

Dugout A three-sided structure in which members of each team sit during a ballgame. Dugouts are located behind first and third base.

Extra Innings The innings played to determine the winner of a game that is tied at the end of the regulation number of innings.

Hot Corner A nickname given to the area of the field near third base that the third baseman must defend.

Jump Term used to describe the running start a baserunner gets when he is trying to steal a base.

Location Term used to describe the accuracy of a pitcher as he works on a hitter. It often refers to pitches within the strike zone.

On Deck Circle A chalk circle near home plate where the next hitter awaits his turn at bat.

Open Stance A term used to describe a batting stance in which the hitter's front foot is further from home plate than his rear foot.

Pickoff A term used when a pitcher tries to throw out a baserunner who has taken a big lead off first, second or third base.

62

Pull Hitter   A hitter who likes to swing early and hit the ball down the lines. A righthanded player will hit to left field and a lefthanded player to right field.

Rubber   The 6″ by 24″ slab of rubber on the mound from which the pitcher pushes off as he throws the ball to home plate.

Sacrifice Bunt   A bunt that the batter hopes will advance a base runner even though he himself is thrown out at first.

Sacrifice Fly   A fly ball that allows a runner to tag up and score from third after the ball is caught for an out.

Safety Squeeze   A bunt with a runner on third. The runner tries to come home only if he feels he can make it.

Steal   A successful advance by a baserunner on a pitched ball that the batter takes for either a ball or strike.

Stop, or **Stretch**   The semi-windup a pitcher takes with runners on base. He must stop for a full second with the ball at his waist before making his delivery to the plate.

Strike Zone   The area over home plate in which a pitch is called a strike even though the batter doesn't swing.

Suicide Squeeze   A bunt attempt with a runner on third base. The runner breaks for home as the ball is pitched and must keep coming even if the batter misses the ball.

Switch Hitter   A batter who can hit from either the left or right side of the plate.

Utility Player   A player without a regular defensive position who can play several different positions in the field when called upon.